BACK OFF! ANIMAL DEFENSES
STINKY ANIMALS

by Nadia Higgins

pogo

Ideas for Parents and Teachers

Pogo Books let children practice reading informational text while introducing them to nonfiction features such as headings, labels, sidebars, maps, and diagrams, as well as a table of contents, glossary, and index.

Carefully leveled text with a strong photo match offers early fluent readers the support they need to succeed.

Before Reading

- "Walk" through the book and point out the various nonfiction features. Ask the student what purpose each feature serves.
- Look at the glossary together. Read and discuss the words.

Read the Book

- Have the child read the book independently.
- Invite him or her to list questions that arise from reading.

After Reading

- Discuss the child's questions. Talk about how he or she might find answers to those questions.
- Prompt the child to think more Ask: Have you seen any of the stinky animals mentioned in the book? Can you think of any stinky animals that aren't discussed?

Pogo Books are published by Jump!
5357 Penn Avenue South
Minneapolis, MN 55419
www.jumplibrary.com

Library of Congress Cataloging-in-Publication Data

Higgins, Nadia, author.
  Stinky animals / by Nadia Higgins.
      pages cm. – (Back off! Animal defenses)
  Audience: Ages 7-10.
  Summary: "Carefully leveled text and vibrant photographs introduce readers to stinky animals such as the skunk, opossum, ladybug, and peccary, and explore how they use bad smells to defend themselves against predators. Includes activity, glossary, and index."
–Provided by publisher.
  Includes index.
  ISBN 978-1-62031-312-1 (hardcover: alk. paper) –
  ISBN 978-1-62496-378-0 (ebook)
  1. Animal chemical defenses–Juvenile literature.
  2. Animal defenses–Juvenile literature.
  3. Adaptation (Biology)–Juvenile literature. I. Title.
  QL759.H4456 2016
  591.47–dc23
                                          2015032609

Series Editor: Jenny Fretland VanVoorst
Series Designer: Anna Peterson
Book Designer: Ellen Schofield
Photo Researcher: Jenny Fretland VanVoorst

Photo Credits: Alamy, 8-9, 11, 20-21; Getty, 10, 13t, 13m; Nature Picture Library, 13b; Shutterstock, cover, 1, 3, 4, 5, 12-13, 14-15, 16, 18-19; SuperStock, 6-7, 17; Thinkstock, 23.

Printed in the United States of America at Corporate Graphics in North Mankato, Minnesota.

TABLE OF CONTENTS

CHAPTER 1

I STINK!

A ladybug crawls in the grass. Any hungry bird could see it.

But look at its bright colors.
Look at its dark spots.
The bug's colors are like
a sign. It says, "I stink!"

If danger comes, smelly yellow
juice oozes from the ladybug's
knees. Yuck! The **predator**
looks for a better snack.

At night, an opossum looks for food in a trash can. Yip-yip! A barking dog **startles** the small animal.

The opossum goes stiff. It closes its eyes and sticks out its tongue. A stinky green liquid leaks out of its bottom.

The opossum looks dead. It smells dead, too. The dog will not bother it now.

DID YOU KNOW?

An opossum does not play dead on purpose. It just happens when the animal gets very scared. It is like fainting or throwing up.

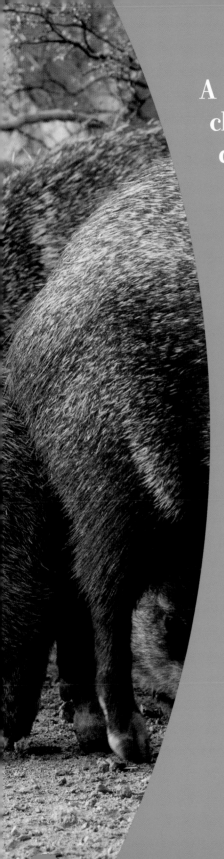

A **peccary** smells like rotten cheese. That is just fine by this desert pig.

Peccaries live in **herds** to stay safe. But they can't see very well. So they rub their smell on each other. That way, they can sniff each other out. Nobody gets left behind.

CHAPTER 2

SMELLY SPRAY

A skunk hisses at a hungry bobcat. The skunk growls and stomps its feet. But the big cat creeps closer.

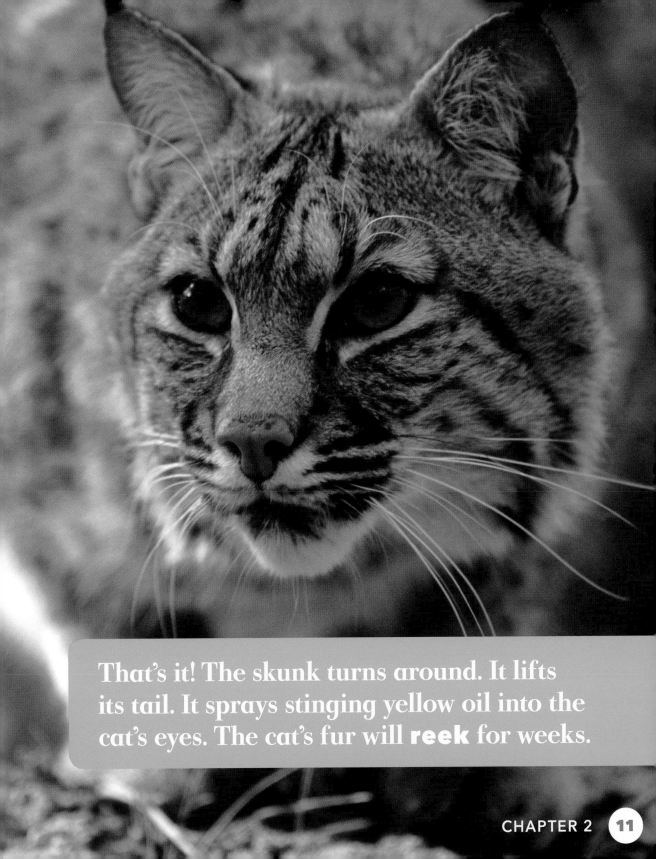

That's it! The skunk turns around. It lifts its tail. It sprays stinging yellow oil into the cat's eyes. The cat's fur will **reek** for weeks.

To spray, a skunk squeezes special **glands** under its tail.

A skunk never gets any mess on its own fur. Even a skunk does not want to smell like a skunk!

TAKE A LOOK!

Each kind of skunk has its own style of spraying.

HOW THEY SPRAY	WHERE THEY LIVE

STRIPED SKUNK

It twists its head to look at its enemy.

HOODED SKUNK

It keeps its back turned.

SPOTTED SKUNK

It does a handstand!

A bombardier beetle sprays its enemies, too. Its spray is boiling hot. Bang! The stinky liquid explodes in its enemy's face.

The spray is hot enough to kill an enemy. But the bug is not harmed at all. How can that be? Scientists are still trying to find out.

CHAPTER 3

· ·

GROSS!

In a **tropical** forest, a Komodo dragon is on the hunt. The giant lizard will eat just about anything. Even a baby Komodo dragon is not safe.

But the baby has a special trick. It rolls in poop. The big lizard is too grossed out to eat it.

Far away in a nest, **hoopoe** chicks sense a cat is near. Together, the baby birds turn their **rumps** toward the enemy.

Ready, aim, fire! They shoot streams of poop in the cat's face. Meow! The cat dashes away from the terrible stink. It will look for less smelly **prey**.

A turkey vulture may be the stinkiest of them all. This large bird eats dead animals. It poops on its feet to cool off.

If you bother it, watch out! This bird throws up on anyone it does not like. It can shoot its rotten, fishy vomit up to 10 feet (3 meters)!

ACTIVITIES & TOOLS

TEST YOUR SENSE OF STINKY

What you call stinky may be OK to someone else. Find out how your sense of stinky matches up with a friend's.

You will need:
- five bowls (or jars or cups)
- five smelly things that fit inside your bowls
- five slips of paper
- something to write with
- a friend

Ideas for stinky stuff:
- a dirty sock
- vinegar
- rubbing alcohol
- a spoon of tuna
- chopped onion or garlic

Steps:

❶ Put one slip of paper next to each bowl. Label each paper so you know which bowl it goes with.

❷ Sniff each bowl one at a time. How stinky is it? Rate the smell from one to five. One means the smell is OK. Three is pretty bad. Five is the worst. Write down your number on the paper that goes with the bowl.

❸ Turn each paper over, so your number is face down.

❹ Now it's your friend's turn to sniff the bowls. Your friend writes on the opposite sides of the papers.

❺ Collect the papers. Compare your numbers with your friend's. Do you and your friend have a similar sense of stinky?

gland: A body part that gives off special substances that the body makes.

herd: A group of animals that live and travel together.

hoopoe: A colorful bird native to Africa and Asia.

peccary: A type of pig that lives in the desert.

predator: An animal that kills other animals for food.

prey: An animal that is killed and eaten by other animals.

reek: To stink really bad.

rump: An animal's rear end.

startle: To surprise someone, but in a scary way.

tropical: Having to do with parts of the world that are hot, humid, and full of green plants.

INDEX

TO LEARN MORE

Learning more is as easy as 1, 2, 3.

1) Go to www.factsurfer.com

2) Enter "stinkyanimals" into the search box.

3) Click the "Surf" button to see a list of websites.

With factsurfer, finding more information is just a click away.